Free-Falling

Into Hell

BY

EVANGELIST HENRY MIRANDA

Free-Falling Into Hell

FREE – FALLING INTO HELL

The Bible makes it quite plain that the consequence for sinning is death. According to Romans 6:23, *the consequence of sin is death, but the gift of God is eternal life through Christ Jesus as our Lord.* Those who choose not to acknowledge Jesus Christ as their personal Lord and Savior will, for their disobedience, spend eternity apart from God, in hell.

Sadly, a lot of people don't take this warning seriously, so they keep sinning even though they know they shouldn't because they think there's still a chance for them to be saved. Nevertheless, the Bible teaches that if we do not acknowledge Jesus Christ as our Lord and Savior, we are doomed to spend eternity in hell.

In *Ephesians 2:1-3*, the apostle Paul writes, *"And you were dead in the trespasses and sins in which you once walked, following the course of this world, following the prince of the power of the air, the spirit that is now at work in the sons of disobedience: among whom we all once lived in the passions of our flesh, carrying out the desires of the body and the mind, and were by nature children of wrath, like the rest of mankind."*

This verse reminds us that apart from Christ, we are spiritually dead in our sins and headed in the direction of destruction. We are the "children of wrath," and as such, defenseless against Satan, who is the prince of the forces of the air. If we reject the free gift of salvation that God offers to us, we are doomed to spend eternity in hell.

John 3:16-18 says, "Because God so loved the world, he gave his only Son, so that whoever believes in him should not perish but have eternal life." God's love for the world led him to make this sacrifice. Because God did not bring his Son into the world in order to judge the world; rather, God sent his Son into the world so that people could be saved through him. Whoever believes in him is not condemned, but whoever does not believe is already condemned, because he has not believed in the name of the only Son of God. "Whoever believes in him is not condemned, but whoever does not believe is already condemned."

This verse is a reminder that God loves us so much that He gave His Son to suffer on the cross for the punishment that we deserve. If we do accept it, we will not be condemned but if we choose not to accept His free gift of salvation, we shall be lost forever. We will be tumbling headfirst into the pits of hell.

If we want to have our sins forgiven, we have to acknowledge Jesus as our Lord and Savior. In the book of *John 14:6*, the Bible declares that *"I am the way, the truth, and the life. No one can approach the Father unless they first come to me."* There is no other method to find salvation in this world.

We do not have the resources to wait any longer. Today is the day that we have to decide to

Free-Falling Into Hell

accept salvation as a gift from God in order to avoid eternal damnation.

Contents

Introduction

Though they are on the steps of the doors to hell, I believe that the unsaved don't want to know God. Everyone has a conscience, which gives an awareness of right and wrong. The Bible says that God has revealed Himself to each individual through their conscience. What more can God do to warn people?

Many are aware of heaven and hell but somehow show no concern. The person who rejects God does not understand the real horrors of this Godless place. This may be because they don't believe hell exists or they are convinced it would be tolerably better than heaven and nothing can be further from the truth.

At this point, they are not preferring hell over God; they are blind to both. They do not perceive the true glories of God, neither do they perceive the true horrors of hell. When they die, they will be shocked beyond words.

What sinners want is not hell but sin. The fact that hell is the inevitable consequence of unforgiven sin does not make the consequence desirable. It is truly not what people want — certainly not what they "want most." Wanting sin is no more equal to wanting hell than wanting chocolate is equal to wanting obesity. However, consuming sin again and again with no regard for repentance will result to eternal damnation.

Some want to believe that God would not send anyone to hell. It is a nice thought, but it is simply unbiblical. God certainly does send people to hell. In His justice, He does pass a sentence and executes it. Indeed, worse than that, God does not just send, He *throws. Revelation 20:15* reads, *"If anyone's name was not found written in the book of life, he was thrown into the lake of fire"* (ESV).

Free-Falling Into Hell

Hell is real. It is a place where many are going but few fully recognize the horrendous fate that awaits them there. It is essential that this truth is not lost but understood and shared.

God

I am not trying to prove anything about God. Neither am I trying to convince you about God. I'm just providing information and it is up to you to believe or not believe that there is a God.

Who is God? No one knows because He is unsearchable. We will never understand God and we shouldn't worry about where God came from or anything about Him. The only information we have about God is what is written in the Bible. If we didn't have the Bible we would not know WHO God Is.

The depth of God's wisdom is unsearchable; no wonder the Bible says that He dwells in an unsearchable light. God is enshrined in mystery and no creature can understand or exhaust who he is. We are only knowledgeable about the dimension of God that is revealed to us, which is something we as human beings need to come to terms with. We cannot understand the depths of God. If we struggle to understand human beings,, what makes you think that you can fully understand a God that is eternal, a God that is everlasting; not bound by space-time or matter? A God who never had a beginning, and will never have an end; a God who is the beginning and who is the end?

Revelation 1:8 (NKJV) says, "I am the Alpha and the Omega, the Beginning and the End, says the Lord, who is and who was and who is to come, the Almighty."

That is where faith comes in. Faith is very important. We accept God's existence as an act of faith.

Hebrews 11:6 (NKJV) says, But without faith it is impossible to please Him, for he who comes to God must believe that He is, and that He is a rewarder of those who diligently seek Him.

Within Christianity, faith, in one sense, is often discussed in terms of believing God's promises, trusting in his faithfulness, and relying on his character and faithfulness to act. Faith speaks the language of the heart. It is an expression of hope that goes beyond the conscious mind. The purpose of faith is to believe in oneself and allow God to come into your life and take control.

The Bible contains a clear definition of faith in *Hebrews 11:1*; *"Now faith is the assurance of things hoped for, the conviction of things not seen."* Simply put, the biblical definition of faith is, "trusting in something you cannot explicitly prove."

This definition of faith contains two aspects: intellectual assent and trust. Intellectual assent is believing something to be true. Trust is actually relying on the fact that something is true. A chair is often used to help illustrate this. Intellectual assent is recognizing that a chair is a chair and agreeing that it is designed to support a person who sits on it. Trust is expressed in actually sitting in the chair.

So many people do not believe there is a God, like I said earlier, but that does not make it so. I believe there is a God and that God has a plan and purpose for humanity.

Can you imagine what it was like in the beginning when there was nothing?

The Trinity

In the beginning, before God created everything there was only the Trinity. The Trinity can be difficult to comprehend from our earthly perspective as human beings. To understand the Trinity, you must have faith. Although the word Trinity is not present in the Bible, Christians know it exists. Christians believe in the Trinity as consisting of the Father, Son, and the Holy Spirit, because Scripture says so.

The father is neither the son nor the Holy Spirit, and the Holy Spirit is neither the son nor the father. The Son is also not the Holy Spirit or the father. Yet the father is God, the son is God, and the Holy Spirit is God. They are three different persons not three separate ways of looking at God, they are all one God.

The Father is God: *Ephesians 1:17* (NKJV) says, "that the God of our Lord Jesus Christ, the Father of glory, may give to you the spirit of wisdom and revelation in the knowledge of Him:"*Philippians 1:2* (NKJV) says, "Grace to you and peace from God our Father and the Lord Jesus Christ."

The Son is God: In *Matthew 1:23* (NKJV) the scripture says, "Behold, the virgin shall be with child, and bear a Son, and they shall call His name Immanuel," which is translated, "God with us." *John 20:28* (NKJV), "And Thomas answered and said to Him, My Lord and my God!"

The Holy Spirit is God: *John 14:26-27* (NKJV) "But the Helper, the Holy Spirit, whom the Father will send in My name, He will teach you all things, and bring to your remembrance all things that I said to you. Peace I leave with you, My peace I give to you; not as the world gives do I give to you. Let not your heart be troubled, neither let it be afraid."

Many Bible scriptures depict the Trinity (all three) fully existing together, and Matthew 3:16-17 is an excellent example; "When He had been baptized, Jesus came up immediately from the water; and behold, the heavens were opened to Him, and He saw the Spirit of God descending like a dove and alighting upon Him. And suddenly a voice came from heaven, saying, This is My beloved Son, in whom I am well pleased."

In the beginning there was no vast universe as we know it today. They were no angels, no creation at all, and many Christians, including many scientists, hold that God created the universe and galaxies, our solar system, and life on earth.

The very first verse of the Scripture, Genesis 1:1(NKJV) says, "In the beginning God created the heavens and the earth." Elsewhere, in *John 1:3* (NKJV), we read, "All things were made through Him, and without Him nothing was made that was made." God had no beginning. He has always existed and he always will. God is infinite: he has no beginning and no end.

Let's take a look at, *Psalm 90:2* (NKJV) which says, "Before the mountains were brought forth, Or ever You had formed the earth and the world, Even from everlasting to everlasting, You are God."

God is so powerful that time and space cannot bind or define Him. God has neither beginning nor end (*Genesis 1:1*). Even the universe had a beginning: the stars, galaxies, and invisible atoms that make up everything in the world, but God had no beginning.

God has never changed or grown old. The Bible says in, *Isaiah 40:28* (NKJV) that, "Have you not known? Have you not heard? The everlasting God, the LORD, The Creator of the ends of the earth, Neither faints nor is weary. His understanding is unsearchable." God is the alpha and omega, the beginning and the end. He has been, and he always will be.

It's impossible for our finite minds to imagine an existence void of time and space limitations. It's like a fish in the sea attempting to comprehend the lifestyle of terrestrial creatures. We tend to impose those limitations on God because we are confined by time and space. Contrary to The Big Bang Theory, God was the one who created the universe, he created all the galaxies and stars. Without God, there is nothing that is made. Once God established the universe, he created the angels.

Colossians 1:16 (NKJV) says, "For by Him all things were created that are in heaven and that are on earth, visible and invisible, whether thrones or dominions or principalities or powers. All things were created through Him and for Him."

Angels

According to Scripture, angels were created. We don't know when they were created, but it appears to have been before the earth was created. They were created before the earth was created, and were made to carry out God's will and serve as messengers.

In the book of Job in the Bible, we can get an idea more or less when the angels were created. God spoke to Job, in *Job 38:4-7* (NKJV) saying; "Where were you when I laid the foundations of the earth? Tell Me, if you have understanding. Who determined its measurements? Surely you know! Or who stretched the line upon it? To what were its foundations fastened? Or who laid its cornerstone, When the morning stars sang together, And all the sons of God shouted for joy?"

Free-Falling Into Hell

In (*Job 38:4,7*), The term "sons of God" is one of the designations for angels, as the Book of Job earlier states. *Job 1:6* (NKJV) says; "Now there was a day when the sons of God came to present themselves before the LORD, and Satan also came among them." If the phrase "sons of God" refers to angels in *Job 38*, then the angels were already in existence before God created the heavens and the earth.

According to the book of Revelation, one of the angels rebelled against God and persuaded one third of the angels to join him.

Revelation 12:7-9 (NKJV), "And war broke out in heaven: Michael and his angels fought with the dragon; and the dragon and his angels fought, but they did not prevail, nor was a place found for them in heaven any longer. So the great dragon was cast out, that old serpent, called the Devil, and Satan, who deceives the whole world; he was cast to the earth, and his angels were cast out with him."

When the rebelling angels were thrown down to this world that we live in the world was void of anything. God had not started His creation in this world.

The Fallen Angel

The angelic world did not have evil angels or demons until there was rebellion in the angelic world, with many angels turning against God and becoming evil. Satan himself led this rebellion. Lucifer was a great angel who rebelled against God and persuaded one third of the angels to side with him. Angels are spirits created by God. The Bible does not give a clear answer as to when angels were created. Cherubims are depicted in Scripture as powerful and majestic angelic creatures who surround God's throne. And Lucifer had once been a guardian cherub.

Revelation 12:7-9 (NKJV), "And war broke out in heaven: Michael and his angels fought with the dragon; and the dragon and his angels fought, but they did not prevail, nor was a place found for them in heaven any longer. So the great dragon was cast out, that serpent of old, called the Devil and

Satan, who deceives the whole world; he was cast to the earth, and his angels were cast out with him."

Since Lucifer had been the model of perfection, what sort of sin led to his fall? His heart became proud because of his incredible beauty. Lucifer allowed his perfection to be the cause of his corruption. He was not satisfied with worshipping God; instead, he wanted to be worshipped. Once a beautiful, powerful angel of God, he lost his former, exalted position in Heaven.

We read in *Ezekiel 28:12-17* (NKJV) that, "Son of man, take up a lamentation for the king of Tyre, and say to him, 'Thus says the Lord GOD: You were the seal of perfection, full of wisdom and perfect in beauty. You were in Eden, the garden of God; every precious stone was your covering: The sardius, topaz, and diamond, Beryl, onyx, and jasper, Sapphire, turquoise, and emerald with gold. The workmanship of your timbrels and pipes was prepared for you on the day you were created. "You were the anointed cherub who covers; I established you; you were on the holy mountain of God; you walked back and forth in the midst of fiery stones. You were perfect in your ways from the day you were created, till iniquity was found in you. By the abundance of your trading you became filled with violence within, and you sinned; therefore I cast you as a profane thing out of the mountain of God; and I destroyed you, O covering cherub, from the midst of the fiery stones. Your heart was lifted up because of your beauty; you corrupted your wisdom for the sake of your splendor; I cast you to the ground, I laid you before kings, that they might gaze at you.'"

The Fallen angels followed Satan's lead instead of God, and together with satan they chose to rebel against God; as they look to Satan as their leader. Prior to the fall, he was an angel of light.

How did Lucifer fall and become Satan? Satan was once named Lucifer, meaning "day star."

The story of his fall is described in two key Old Testament chapters – *Ezekiel 28* and *Isaiah 14*.

In the second chapter of the Bible, we are told that God created the heavens, earth, and everything in them. The Bible also indicates that angels were created while the earth was still not formed, even before human life was created. Therefore, the first creation by God was the supreme archangel, followed by other archangels, who are identified with lower intellects. Lucifer fell because of pride. He desired to be God, not to be a servant of God. Notice the many "I will..." statements in *Isaiah 14:12-15*.

Ezekiel 28:12-15 describes Satan as an exceedingly beautiful angel. Satan was likely the highest of all angels, the anointed cherub, the most beautiful of all of God's creation, but he was not content with his position. Instead, Satan desired to be God, to essentially "kick God off His throne" and take over the rule of the universe. He wanted to be

God, and that is specifically why Satan tempted Adam and Eve in the Garden of Eden (*Genesis 3:1-5*).

Lucifer became so impressed with his own beauty, intelligence, power, and position that he began to desire for himself the honor and glory that belonged to God alone. This pride marked the beginning of sin in the universe.

The Devil, also referred to as Satan, is best known as the personification of evil and the nemesis of good people everywhere. His image and story have evolved over the years. He has been called many different names in various cultures: Beelzebub, Lucifer, Satan, and Mephistopheles, to name a few, with various physical descriptions including horns and hooved feet. But this malevolent being and his legion of demons continues to strike fear in people from all walks of life as the antithesis of all things good.

Although the Devil is present in some form in many religions and can be compared to some mythological gods, he's arguably best known for his role in Christianity. In modern biblical translations, the Devil is the adversary of God and God's people.

How did Satan fall from heaven? A fall is not an accurate description; it would be far more accurate to say God cast Satan out of heaven as the scripture says in (*Isaiah 14:15; Ezekiel 28:16-17*). Satan did not fall from heaven; instead, he was cast out.

If we use the Bible as our authority, then the Devil looks nothing like we can imagine. His name originally was Lucifer, and he was described as a bright morning star. Satan was the greatest of all of God's creation. The greatest of all the angels and the most powerful being that God has ever created, including any human being ever made. When God created him, there was nothing like him in the entire universe and all of God's creation. Satan's fall from heaven is symbolically described in Isaiah 14:12-14 and Ezekiel 28:12-18. While these two passages refer specifically to the kings of Babylon and Tyre, they also reference the spiritual power behind those kings, namely, Satan. These passages describe why Satan fell, but they did not specifically point out when the fall occurred. What we do know is this: angels were created before the earth (*Job 38:4-7*). Satan fell before he tempted Adam and Eve in the Garden (*Genesis 3:1-14*).

Therefore, Satan's fall must have occurred somewhere after the angels were created and before he tempted Adam and Eve in the Garden of Eden. Scripture does not specifically say whether Satan's fall occurred hours, days, or years before he tempted Adam and Eve in the Garden.

The book of Job tells us that Satan still had access to heaven and the throne of God, at least at that time. "One day, the angels came to present themselves before the LORD, and Satan also came with them. The LORD said to Satan, 'Where have you come from?' Satan answered the Lord, 'From roaming through the earth and going back and forth on it'" (Job 1:6-7). Apparently, at that time, Satan was still moving freely between heaven and earth, speaking to God directly and answering for his activities. Whether God has discontinued this access is a matter of debate. Some say Satan's access to heaven was ended at the death of Christ. Others believe Satan's access to heaven will end at the end of the war in heaven.

The devil hasn't always existed; he had a beginning, and someday his work will come to an end. Only God is eternal. Satan has since his casting out continued to oppose God and lead people astray, and he will continue to do so until the end of time when he will be bound forever and ever (see Revelation 20:10). Don't be deceived by his temptations, no matter how attractive they seem!

Free-Falling Into Hell

Never doubt that the devil is real or powerful, but he is also a defeated foe. By His death and resurrection, Jesus Christ overcame the powers of sin and death and hell. Be certain of your commitment to Christ, for when we give our lives to Him, God frees us from Satan's grip and makes us part of His family forever. The Bible's words are true: The reason that God sent His only son to earth was to become the sacrifice that paid for all our sins. Without Jesus, no man or woman could enter heaven because we are all stained with sin. On the other hand, if we believe in Christ, we can have eternal life in heaven.

Why didn't God kill or destroy Satan when he rebelled? If God had destroyed Satan immediately, the angels would have begun to serve Him from fear rather than from love. This would have defeated the very purpose He had in creating beings with the power of choice (free will) in the first place. That's why he was allowed to make his pitch to Adam and

Eve. This planet has become a testing ground where the character of Satan and the nature of his kingdom are contrasted with the character of God and the nature of His kingdom.

God can destroy Satan and sin. He will also have to destroy those who stubbornly resist His grace and cling to Satan's alternatives. God is just as anxious to resolve the problem of sin and suffering as we are to have Him do so. But He is waiting until He can do it permanently and until He can both preserve our free will and prevent evil from ever appearing again.

Lucifer originated the First Sin, "Pride."

Creation and The Fall

Ephesians 2:10 (NKJV) *"For we are His workmanship, created in Christ Jesus for good works, which God prepared beforehand that we should walk in them".*

God's Original Plan for Us

God's original plan for mankind was for us to enjoy life and have fellowship with Him and to partake of His blessings. He designed the world so that we would enjoy our life on earth for eternity.

Genesis 2:7-9 (NKJV) "And the LORD God formed man of the dust of the ground, and breathed into his nostrils the breath of life; and man became a living being. The LORD God planted a garden eastward in Eden, and there He put the man whom He had formed. And out of the ground the LORD God made every tree grow that is pleasant to the sight and good for food. The tree of life was also in the midst of the garden, and the tree of the knowledge of good and evil."

God created a paradise, a perfect, exquisite, and lush garden filled with all manner of God's special treats. Every tree was unique in its shape, vibrant color, and each with its own distinctive and delectable fruit. It must have been a breathtaking wonderland for Adam to wander through and visually take in the magnificence, smell all the fragrances, and taste the sweetness of all the different fruits, each in their original uncontaminated state. Eden was a garden planted explicitly by God. It was a place God made to be a perfect habitation for the beginning of humanity.

Genesis 2:15-17 (NKJV) says, "Then the LORD God took the man and put him in the garden of Eden to tend and keep it. And the LORD God commanded the man, saying, "Of every tree of the garden you may freely eat; but of the tree of the knowledge of good and evil you shall not eat, for in the day that you eat of it you shall surely die."

Free-Falling Into Hell

Consider God's statement here in *verse 16-17*: "You are free to eat from any tree in the garden; but you must not eat from the tree of the knowledge of good and evil, for when you eat of it, you will surely die."

Everything was good until Satan, the fallen angel, came into the picture. When God put Adam and Eve in the Garden of Eden, they were both innocent and pure. Satan came disguised as a snake and spoke to Eve, convincing her to eat the fruit from the tree of good and evil. Eve told the serpent that God said they should not eat it for they would die if they did, but Satan tempted Eve to eat, saying that she would become like God if she did. Eve believed the lie and picked the forbidden fruit and took a bite of the fruit. She then gave some to Adam for him to eat. Their eyes were opened, and their innocence was lost. Now that they had sinned, Adam and Eve immediately felt ashamed and tried to hide from God.

After they sinned in (*Genesis 3:19*), God sentenced them to die as per *Genesis 2:17*. That is why they were removed from the Garden of Eden. Had they eaten from the Tree of Life they would have lived forever. Which was partly why they were forbidden from eating from the tree. They had already eaten of the Tree Of Knowledge of Good and Evil. So, God made sure they did not eat from the Tree of Life.

Genesis 3:24 (NKJV) says, "So He drove out the man; and He placed cherubim at the east of the garden of Eden, and a flaming sword which turned every way, to guard the way to the tree of life."

After the rebellion of Adam and Eve, the world was in a fallen state and suffered the degrading and deadly spiritual, moral, and social consequences of sinfulness. From friendship with God to estrangement from Him, and enmity with Him has left us diseased and dying in every part of our body.

Free-Falling Into Hell

God created this world, and He created man to have fellowship with Him. Instead, man chose to go his own way when he disobeyed God's instructions in the garden, and the true fellowship with God was broken.

This self-will is still evident today. It is exhibited by an attitude of active rejection or passive indifference. This behavior is what God's Word calls sin. Adam had the privilege of purity and perfection. God had given him dominion over all creation. He was the appointed caretaker over all living creatures, and all the garden was also under his management. He had a job that kept him busy because planting was already finished. The weather was mild, the river irrigated the garden sufficiently, and everything was producing perfectly. God would visit them in the cool of the day.

This time, however, instead of going out to meet God, they hid themselves from the presence of God. What a sad change because before they sinned, if they had heard the voice of God coming, they probably would have run out to meet Him in a humble, joyous welcome for His gracious visits.

But now, God had become a terror to them. They hid from God because their intimate fellowship with Him was broken. Shame leads to fear and alienation. They wanted the knowledge of good and evil, which they were inclined to believe would make them divine. They got that knowledge they sought but they lost the power to do right. The knowledge of evil made them sad and the knowledge of good made them terrified. Before the fall, Adam and Eve had uninterrupted fellowship with God, but the relationship was vastly changed after they sinned.

When Adam was placed in the Garden of Eden, he was supposed to subdue the earth. This would mean warfare; it means to tread down and subjugate. This implied existence of an enemy that Adam was to conquer. The only enemy around at that time and still with us today was Lucifer, also known as Satan, the devil. Conquering Satan would have made the whole world like a part of the Garden of Eden.

Hope in Jesus

Adam lost his rights to the dominion of this world. That is why Jesus being God had to come down and reclaim the rights that Adam had lost. The only way that we could reconcile with God is through the spirit. When Jesus died on the cross, he reclaimed the rights that Adam had lost. We have the choice to turn away from sin and turn to God.

We can't do anything to earn our way into heaven, but the good news is that we don't have to. God sent Jesus into the world, and He lived the way we were always meant to live. Jesus came to provide the only way by which we could be reunited with God. His innocent death took the punishment we deserve because of our rejection of God.

Because Jesus has paid the price for us, he offers us salvation and eternal life. Make a decision to accept Jesus into your lives and to share eternity with him. Adam's sin hindered us from receiving all that God has for us, but Jesus made it possible for us to get back paradise and to have God's original plan for our lives. His original plan was for us to enjoy our life on earth and enjoy personal communion and fellowship with Him. His original desire to bless us has never changed. Jesus taught that there is a real heaven and a real hell.

Every person is either bound for heaven or hell. Every person is headed for a destination that is permanent and eternal. Where a person will spend eternity depends on whether that person receives Jesus Christ or rejects Him. Once a person dies, his eternal destiny remains unchanged. As Christians, we must remember that we live by faith and every word that proceeds from our Father. Who are we to question how, where, or when things were done?

Free-Falling Into Hell

We know that Adam sinned, and mankind became sinners ruled by Satan, the prince of this world. The only way man could be reconciled back to God would be if he were bought back with a price. The debt was paid. Jesus paid our debt with the shedding of His blood on the cross.

Everybody has a choice to use their free will to either follow God's purpose or his own purpose. The big picture is that man, in his own strengths, cannot follow the commandments of God. We need help because we are weak, and our desires take us away from God. With His infinite mercies, God provided that help through his Son, Jesus Christ, who gave His life so that we can be reconciled to God if we so choose.

Contrary to different beliefs, there is only one road that leads to God: Jesus Christ. Satan does not want to allow us to walk that road. He will do whatever it takes to convince you that you are wasting your time and there is no God. Satan hates

God and will use us to hurt God. We must remember that Satan has already been defeated, and the only power he has over us is what we allow him to have. *"Greater is He that is in you than he that is in the world."*

Christianity is not like other religions; it is based on the death of Jesus Christ, whereas all other religions base their claim to greatness on the life and teaching of those who founded them. The Gospel of Jesus Christ centers on the person of Jesus Christ, especially his death at Calvary. Because of his death, the price was paid for our redemption. Through the death of the Son of God himself, Jesus Christ, we have forgiveness for our sins and the promise of eternal life.

The devil comes to steal, kill, and destroy. Satan is not your friend, but he pretends that he is, and he will do whatever it takes to keep you from God. We once were of this world and a friend to the devil. But now, we belong to God and are friends of

God. The devil does not like losing his own and will try every trick he knows to turn you away from God. That's where spiritual warfare comes in. Satan will do whatever it takes to keep this world in darkness. He is totally against anything that God has planned for us. He is a great imitator.

Fortunately, through Christ we have a better destiny, that of Eden restored. We hope our destiny is to be with God in heaven like Adam and Eve were in the garden. After the fall, man's destination became certain; we are all marching to the grave! The funeral homes and the cemeteries prove this statement. All men are headed for that final day of death. However, if we choose Christ, we can go to the grave with the hope of eternal life when he, Jesus, comes to save his own from death and the grave.

Evangelist Henry Miranda

Total Depravity

The doctrine of total depravity asserts that as a result of the fall people are not inclined or even able to love God wholly with their heart, mind, and strength, but rather are inclined by nature to serve their own will, desires and to reject his rule.

Depravity is the Biblical teaching that humanity since the Fall has inherited both the guilt and sinful nature of Adam in such a way that absolutely everything about them is affected by sin. As a consequence of man's fall, every person born into the world is enslaved to the service of sin as a result of their fallen nature and, apart from the efficacious (irresistible) or prevenient (enabling) grace of God, is completely unable to choose by themselves to follow God or refrain from evil.

Rebellion is opposition to authority. It always begins in the heart. Rebellion against God's authority was humanity's first sin and continues to be its downfall. Our sinful nature does not want to bow to the authority of another, even God. We want to be our own bosses, and that rebellion in the human heart is the root of all sin (*Romans 3:23*).

Because of the fall of Adam, everyone is born with a sinful nature; wicked or immoral. Christian doctrine holds that humanity, through birth, inherits a tainted nature with a proclivity to sinful conduct.

The sinful nature is described in *Galatians 5:19-26* (NKJV), *"Now the works of the flesh are evident, which are: adultery, fornication, uncleanness, lewdness, idolatry, sorcery, hatred, contentions, jealousies, outbursts of wrath, selfish ambitions, dissensions, heresies, envy, murders, drunkenness, revelries, and the like; of which I tell you beforehand, just as I also told you in time past, that those who practice such things will not inherit the kingdom of God. But the fruit of the Spirit is love, joy, peace, long-suffering, kindness, goodness, faithfulness, gentleness, and self-control. Against such there is no law. And those who are Christ's have crucified the flesh with its passions and desires. If we live in the Spirit, let us also walk in the Spirit. Let us not become conceited, provoking one another, envying one another."*

The sinful nature is the reason why most people are going to go to Hell. All mankind sins as soon as they are capable of moral action. The secular world we live in today promotes rebellion. People don't want to listen to authority. People want to be the god of their own lives; in rebellion against God.

Jesus didn't die for your sins so you can live in rebellion and spit on God's grace. The, *"we're all sinners"* excuse does not justify living in darkness. The dead can't raise themselves. In the same way, there is nothing a fallen man can do to save himself. He is absolutely helpless. He can't expect his rational mind to help him overcome moral or spiritual corruption. His thoughts, his will and emotions are not naturally directed toward God. In a strictly theological sense, he is "totally depraved." He bears the stain of sin in every part of his being.

There are many ways to live in rebellion such as living a lifestyle of sin, refusing God's calling, trusting ourselves rather than trusting in the Lord, being unforgiving, and more. In *1 Samuel 15:23*, God said rebellion is as the sin of witchcraft. Rebellion is an attitude displayed to contradict the authority and it started from the beginning of Creation. When God created Adam and Eve, He put them in the Garden of Eden and gave them instructions on what to do and what not to do.

Now, because of the fall of man, and because of this act of disobedience all mankind have a sinful nature. *Romans 5:12* (NKJV) says; "Therefore, just as through one man sin entered the world, and death through sin, and thus death spread to all men because all have sinned." We all possess a sinful nature that we inherited from Adam. Whether we like it or not, that is the way it is! We are all born sinners and must die because we come from Adam.

The first man who disobeyed God's commandment is our forefather and we are just like him. Who among us can say he has never disobeyed the commandments of God? Not a single one of us! Like a horrible contagious disease, the sin that was in Adam has spread to us all just as an epidemic is not confined to the one from whom it originates.

What exactly is sin anyway? The truth is that sin, as defined in the original translations of the Bible, means "to miss the mark." The mark, in this case, is the standard of perfection established by God and evidenced by Jesus. Viewed in that light, it is clear that we are all sinners. The good news in all of this is that once we recognize ourselves as sinners, we need to only repent and embrace Jesus to be forgiven.

Jesus can forgive us because He died and rose again three days later in victory over sin and death.

Sin caused man's separation from God. However, God loves us so much that He provides for us the way back into good fellowship with Him through Jesus Christ. His steadfast love and kindness leads us back to repentance, and in His grace and mercy forgives us of all our sins even though none of us deserves this forgiveness. No one can earn forgiveness and reconciliation with God. It is a free gift to those who believe and accept it by faith. Sin is an offense or rebellion against God. It is what separates us from God.

Remember that to stay in a state of rebellion is death. The devil stays busy at work keeping us in sin and away from God. Yet, those who continue to live in this state of rebellion against God have not lost their opportunity to be God's child. All they need do is to repent. We don't have to sin. We sin by choice. You must want to serve God with all your heart, body, and soul to stay away from sin. A desire to sin is simply a way of expressing your disbelief that God's way is best. God gave us free will and we must decide on our own how we want to lead our life.

The world's way was easy, and we fell into its trap. The world is good at presenting a great and enticing illusion of its goodness. God gave us the choice to either serve Him or the prince of this world, the devil. There is no excuse for sin. Man has always had the opportunity to know God and do His will according to the light of nature and conscience. From the very first sin, it has been a matter of willfulness. No one can say, "I could not help it." Remember that, *"No temptation has overtaken you except what is common to mankind. And God is faithful; he will not let you be tempted beyond what you can bear. But when you are tempted, he will also provide a way out so that you can endure it." 1 Corinthians 10:13.*

The Reality of Hell

Jesus gives more vivid detail of hell than He does of heaven. He talked about it more, too. There's no denying it, Jesus knew, believed, and warned against the absolute reality of hell.

Have you ever wondered what happens to us after we die?

Heaven Is a Real Place

According to the Bible, heaven is a real place populated with real people. Those who go there enter through a real gate, travel on real streets, and live in real buildings. They have new, perfected bodies and recieve eternal rewards.

All of these things are wonderful but the best attribute of heaven is that God lives there. *Revelation 22:3* (NKJV) states, "There shall be no more curse, but the throne of God and of the Lamb shall be in it, and His servants shall serve Him". All who live in heaven will be in God's presence, never again to experience the curse that came with the fall of man.

Hell Is Also Real

Hell is also a real place populated with real people. The Bible depicts hell as a bottomless pit, a place of sorrow filled with torment and the sounds of wailing and gnashing of teeth. The inhabitants of hell experience loneliness and regret. There is no escape. By reading Jesus' account of the rich man and Lazarus in *Luke 16:19-31*, we can see that anyone already in hell would not want any of their loved ones joining them there.

Also, *Matthew 25:41* makes it clear that hell's everlasting fire was never intended for people, but was "prepared for the devil and his angels." *Psalm 9:17* shows us that hell is a place for the wicked and the nations that forget God. Those who know the truth and disobey it are also destined for hell. But it is not the wicked or disobedient man's sin that sends him to hell, it is his rejection of Jesus Christ. As *John 3:18* states, "He who believes in Him is not condemned; but he who does not believe is condemned already, because he has not believed in the name of the only begotten Son of God."

Jesus came to give man the opportunity to escape condemnation. During His time on earth, He not only reference hell, but He described it in great detail.

A Place of Eternal Torment

We see in *Luke 16:23* which says, "And being in torments in Hades, he lifted up his eyes and saw Abraham afar off, and Lazarus in his bosom."

Unquenchable Fire

Mark 9:43 states. "If your hand causes you to sin, cut it off. It is better for you to enter into life maimed, rather than having two hands, to go to hell, into the fire that shall never be quenched."

Where The Worm Does Not Die

Mark 9:48 says, "Their worm does not die, And the fire is not quenched." It is where people will gnash their teeth in anguish and regret.

Matthew 13:42, "...and will cast them into the furnace of fire. There will be wailing and gnashing of teeth." From which there is no return, even to warn loved ones.

Luke 16:19-31:

"There was a certain rich man who was clothed in purple and fine linen and fared sumptuously every day. But there was a certain beggar named Lazarus, full of sores, who was laid at his gate, desiring to be fed with the crumbs which fell from the rich man's table. Moreover, the dogs came and licked his sores. So it was that the beggar died, and was carried by the angels to Abraham's bosom. The rich man also died and was buried. And being in torments in Hades, he lifted up his eyes and saw Abraham afar off, and Lazarus in his bosom. Then he cried and said, 'Father Abraham, have mercy on me, and send Lazarus that he may dip the tip of his finger in water and cool my tongue; for I am tormented in this flame.' But Abraham said, 'Son, remember that in your lifetime you received your good things, and likewise Lazarus evil things; but now he is comforted and you are tormented. And besides all this, between us and you there is a great gulf fixed, so that those who want to pass from here to you cannot, nor can those from there pass to us.' Then he said, 'I beg you therefore, father, that you would send him to my father's house, for I have five brothers, that he may testify to them, lest they also come to this place of torment.'

Abraham said to him, 'They have Moses and the prophets; let them hear them.' And he said, 'No, father Abraham; but if one goes to them from the dead, they will repent.' But he said to him, 'If they do not hear Moses and the prophets, neither will they be persuaded though one rise from the dead.'"

A Place Of "Outer Darkness"

Matthew 25:30, "And cast the unprofitable servant into the outer darkness. There will be weeping and gnashing of teeth."

Comparing It To "Gehenna"

Gehenna was a trash dump outside the walls of Jerusalem where rubbish was burned and maggots abounded. *Matthew 10:28* reads, "And do not fear those who kill the body but cannot kill the soul. But rather fear Him who is able to destroy both soul and body in hell."

God intended to fellowship with us in a flawless world. This changed when Eve succumbed to Satan's temptations, followed by Adam. Satan is full of deceit. When he approached Eve in the garden, disguised as a serpent, he knew that if Adam and Eve ate of the tree of knowledge, they would ingest the poison of his evil nature and be corrupted by sin and death forever.

Because they both partook of the forbidden fruit, they were expelled from Paradise. Since that day, man has attempted to re-establish their relationship with God that has been lost. However, they do it in their own way.

God too, has a plan to restore this lost fellowship. However, His plan is different from the one that we would naturally come up with. He sent His Son to be a perfect sacrifice for the rest of humanity. When Jesus went to the cross, He carried the sins of the entire world on His shoulders. This act gives mankind the opportunity to reclaim the lost fellowship between God and His creation.

God has graciously placed within each of us a conscience, an inner sense of right and wrong. Deep down, we know heaven and hell aren't illusions. Our conscience gives us an awareness of them as we discern between good and evil. Paul writes in *Romans 2:14-15* that, "For when Gentiles, who do not have the law, by nature do the things in the law, these, although not having the law, are a law to themselves, who show the work of the law written in their hearts, their conscience also bearing witness, and between themselves their thoughts accusing or else excusing them."

Some people believe that the only heaven or hell anyone will ever experience is here on earth. Still, others don't know what to believe. Everyone needs to know the truth about heaven and hell because, according to *1 Thessalonians 5:23*, each of us has a spirit and a soul as well as a body. When our physical body dies, our spirit will live somewhere forever. We have a choice between heaven and hell while we are alive because once we die, it will be too late.

By faith, we know that heaven is a real place. Those who go there enter through the narrow gate.

They will forever be free from sin and its curse, which manifests in pain and sickness. Those in heaven can experience joyous reunions with friends and loved ones who also chose heaven. But most important of all, God is there.

Revelation 22:3 says, "And there shall be no more curse, but the throne of God and of the Lamb shall be in it, and His servants shall serve Him." All who live in heaven will be in God's presence, never again experiencing the curse that came with the fall of man. The true reality of humanity's original destiny, and pure fellowship with God, will be restored.

You Don't Need Satan's Help

You are well on the way to hell all by yourself unless you repent of your ways and turn to the truth, which is God's truth. You don't need the devil's help to get to hell. You are doing a fine job on your own. The devil is only there to assist you on your journey to hell, and he wants to ensure you don't get lost along the way. The only goal that the devil has is to keep us from establishing a relationship with God. If he fails and we come to know God, then the devil tries to keep us from growing and developing a deeper relationship with God. The devil desires to keep us from experiencing God's love in our lives and from having God's presence in our lives. He wants to stop God's power that is actively at work in us when we belong to God.

The Bible tells us that God created the devil as a cherub, the most powerful of God's angelic beings. Sometime after his creation and before the creation of mankind, the devil rebelled against God and took one-third of the angels with him into rebellion.

God assuredly included this information that some angels have departed from Him, for it tells us that the angels that stayed with Him are praising God and serving Him and are doing this at their own free will.

The devil is a fallen angel who rebelled against God. He is often identified as the serpent in the Garden of Eden, whose persuasions lead to two corresponding Christian doctrines. One is "the original sin," which is the disobedience of Adam, and the other is "the Redemption of Jesus Christ," which in turn brings us to a relationship with God.

God placed Adam and Eve in the garden for two main reasons. The first was to have fellowship with them while enjoying an exchange of love. The second was to test their competency. God is not a tyrant or a dictator; He does not force Himself on us. God let Adam experience the consequences of their actions. Had Adam not disobeyed God, there would be no sin in nature. That brings us to the question, "Why did God create sin"?

God did not create sin. He only allowed it. We may contemplate why God permitted sin, but beyond that, the subject is incomprehensible and must be left in the hands of God. Martin Luther said, "This is so high that no other answer can be given than that, so it has pleased God." God, in His Omniscience, knew that Eve and Adam would sin, and he could have stopped it, since he is Omnipotent, but he did not. God's only part in allowing sin into the world was that he led man to experience the consequences of his actions. If Adam and Eve had not disobeyed God, there would be no sinful nature.

God knew that Adam and Eve would fail, and so he made provisions for it in eternity past. Sin was included in God's plan, and man is responsible for it, yet God always has control over sin.

"But with the precious blood of Christ, as of a lamb without blemish and without spot. He indeed was foreordained before the foundation of the world, but was manifest in these last times for you who through Him believe in God, who raised Him from the dead and gave Him glory, so that your faith and hope are in God." (1 *Peter 1:19-21* NKJV).

God did not warn Adam and Eve that they would be separated from Him; He warned them that they would be physically and spiritually dead. Spiritually dead is separation from God. God's point is that we are spiritually dead until we accept Jesus as our Lord and Savior. We cannot understand spiritual truths not until we believe the truth about Jesus and are willing to yield ourselves to Him.

The separation between God and mankind exists because God is perfect, and mankind is imperfect. One imperfection we all share as human beings is selfishness. Selfishness is a cornerstone emotion that governs all of our actions. Despite

Free-Falling Into Hell

God's warning, Adam and Eve were kicked out by the gardener because they wanted what they wanted. This is the original sin, disobedience due to willful selfishness. Willful selfishness is the source of evil in our world and a sort of separation between God and us.

"Behold, the Lord's hand is not shortened, That it cannot save; Nor His ear heavy, That it cannot hear. But your iniquities have separated you from your God; And your sins have hidden His face from you, So that He will not hear. For your hands are defiled with blood, And your fingers with iniquity; Your lips have spoken lies, Your tongue has muttered perversity" (*Isaiah 59:1-3* NKJV).

The reason God permitted sin was to allow us to have a free choice between good and evil. This can only be possible if sin is present. God created us to have fellowship with Him, but He warned us to choose for ourselves whether we wanted to fellowship with Him or not. God could have created beings who would do his bidding, but that would mean they would have to be mindless with no will of their own.

The Narrow Road

People are always looking for churches that have watered-down the gospel or the seeker-friendly churches (seeker churches have become one of the fastest-growing religious movements in the country). They are there to please the people and not teach the Gospel.

Sometimes we quit before we get to our destination. I remember when I was nine, my dad called and asked me to meet him to help him sell his watermelons. He told me to get on the bus and get off on a certain street. I got on the bus but after only a short ride I alighted. I can't really remember why, all I know is that I never got to my destination and needless to say, my dad was upset. Sometimes we quit too soon when God is working in our lives. We need to give God a chance to complete the work he is doing in us. Remember, God has only the best in mind for you.

Luke 13:23-25 (NKJV) reads; *"Then one said to Him, "Lord, are there few who are saved?" And He said to them, "Strive to enter through the narrow gate, for many, I say to you, will seek to enter and will not be able. When once the Master of the house has risen up and shut the door, and you begin to stand outside and knock at the door, saying, 'Lord, Lord, open for us,' and He will answer and say to you, 'I do not know you, where you are from,'"*

"But know this, that in the last days perilous times will come: For men will be lovers of themselves, lovers of money, boasters, proud, blasphemers, disobedient to parents, unthankful, unholy, unloving, unforgiving, slanderers, without self-control, brutal, despisers of good, traitors, headstrong, haughty, lovers of pleasure rather than lovers of God, having a form of godliness but denying its power. And from such people turn away! **2Timothy 3:1-5 NKJV.**

Free-Falling Into Hell

I Timothy 4:1-3 NKJV says; "Now the Spirit expressly says that in latter times some will depart from the faith, giving heed to deceiving spirits and doctrines of demons, speaking lies in hypocrisy, having their own conscience seared with a hot iron, forbidding to marry, and commanding to abstain from foods which God created to be received with thanksgiving by those who believe and know the truth."

Jesus makes it clear that we all stand at the crossroads, and there are two paths in front of us. The wide path leads to hell. The second, narrow path leads to eternal life in heaven. The narrow road is difficult; the wide road is easy. Anyone who tells you that following Christ is easy is lying. I'll tell you what's easy: Going with the flow, following the crowd, doing what everyone else is doing. It's the path of least resistance, and it's so, so easy. But following Jesus on the narrow path to heaven is never easy.

The narrow road is long; the wide road is short. Traveling the wide road to destruction is not only easy, it's short, so short that you're already there. The Bible makes it clear that if you don't have Jesus in your heart, you are already dead in your sins. You're not on our way to destruction you are already there.

The shortest road in the world is the road to hell. You don't need to exert an ounce of effort to get there because you have already made your reservation. But the road to heaven is a long road. As Christians, we may have come a long way in our faith, but we still have a long way to go. However hard it is to follow Christ well over the long haul, it is worth it.

The road to Heaven is extremely small and most people will not find it. Many people say they love Christ, but their actions show that they truly hate Him. Just because you go to church doesn't mean you're going to go to Heaven.

Free-Falling Into Hell

Most people will tell you, "I don't care if I am heading to hell, I hate God." People in hell hate God, they don't cry out to God to help them they curse God. People in hell still hate God.

Have you ever wondered if Adam loved God, what about Eve, what was Adam's heart's condition towards God?

God is holy and never makes any mistakes, so only through Jesus can we be perfect. People have so many ways to worship different gods, but is not the right God! There is no reason not to go to Heaven because God gives you every opportunity. If you love the Lord you will commit to Him. You only have one chance. It's either Paradise or torment. God is good and a good judge must punish the guilty. Whoever wants to keep their life will lose it. Stop being part of the world, deny yourself, and take up the cross daily.

When God created Lucifer and Adam, they were both innocent and without a sinful nature. The only thing they had in common was a free will to be able to choose and on their own without any interference from God.

Here is the question: Why did they both rebel against God?

The one thing that Lucifer and Adam had in common was both were created with no wrong because there was no sin yet. But yet they both rebelled.

People don't want to hear about God. But there is no excuse to not know God. *Hebrews 10:16* (NKJV) says, "This is the covenant that I will make with them after those days, says the LORD: I will put My laws into their hearts, and in their minds, I will write them."

We have the Holy Spirit convicts us. The atheist doesn't believe in God, so they say, but if they don't believe in God, how can they hate something that they don't believe in?

Free-Falling Into Hell

Everyone has rebelled against God. People sin because by nature, they are sinners'. Men are born in sin, so man hates God because God is good. They can't stand good because they like doing things in darkness. Why do men hate God's laws? It is because it is good, and people have no fear of God, no reverence.

In the beginning God created everything! Everything we know about creation was written in the Bible by men directed by the Holy Spirit. We must take everything by faith. "Faith means; belief, firm persuasion, assurance, firm conviction, faithfulness." Faith is confidence in what we hope for and the assurance that the lord is working, even though we cannot see it. Faith knows that no matter the situation in our lives or someone else's, the lord is working on it.

The Bible teaches that "faith is being sure of what we hope for and certain of what we do not see" (*Hebrews 11:1*). So, faith is being certain about the realities we believe are true but we cannot see with our physical eyes. God's Word also says that "without faith it is impossible to please God…" (*Hebrews 11:6*).

In Genesis we see that God said everything was good and then we have the fall in the garden of Eden. Nothing was good after that and the sinful nature was born. Hate remained in the earth not love. Look at the story of Noah's generation and how God destroyed the people.

In *1 Corinthians 6:9* (NKJV) it says, "Do you not know that the unrighteous will not inherit the kingdom of God? Do not be deceived. Neither fornicators, nor idolaters, nor adulterers, nor homosexuals, nor sodomites," "John 10:1 (NKJV) tell us that, "Most assuredly, I say to you, he who does not enter the sheepfold by the door, but climbs up some other way, the same is a thief and a robber."

Free-Falling Into Hell

The Gate

John 10: 6-9 says, "Jesus used this figure of speech, but the pharisees did not understand what he was telling them. Therefore, Jesus said again, "I tell you the truth, I am the gate for the sheep. All who ever came before me were thieves and robbers, but the sheep did not listen to them. I am the gate; whoever enters through me will be saved.""

Most people that say the sinner's prayer, "Jesus, I know that I am a sinner, and I ask for Your forgiveness. I believe You died for my sins and rose from the dead. I turn from my sins and invite You to come into my heart and life. I want to trust and follow You as my Lord and Savior." don't make a complete change in their lives; they continue the way they were. It's like this when you asked Jesus into your heart you walk through the gate, but you stop on the other side and that's as far as you will go. In the other hand, a true born-again Christian will start their walk on the narrow road on the other side of the gate.

The bible says in *Matthew 25:41* (NKJV) that, "Then He will also say to those on the left hand, 'Depart from Me, you cursed, into the everlasting fire prepared for the devil and his angels:"

Salvation Is A Free Choice

The Bible presents us with the opportunity to choose freely between salvation and eternal damnation. *Ephesians 2:8-9* states, "For by grace you have been saved through faith, and that not of yourselves; it is the gift of God, not of works, lest anyone should boast." This is in reference to the fact that Christians are saved by grace. This text reminds us that salvation is a free gift from God and not something that we can earn through our own efforts. Instead, it is something that we get as a gift from God. It is up to each one of us to make the appropriate choice regarding this free gift of salvation that God offers to us, but we have the option to either embrace it or reject it.

Additionally, the Bible instructs us that believing in Jesus Christ is the only way to be saved. It is written in *Romans 10:9-10* that, "you will be saved if you confess with your mouth the Lord Jesus and believe in your heart that God has raised Him from the dead...." Because believing in one's heart leads to virtuous living, and confessing one's sins via one's tongue leads to being saved. According to what is stated in this passage, in order for us to be saved, we need to have trust in Jesus and confess that we believe in Him.

It is essential not to forget that salvation is not something we can get through our own efforts. Because, salvation is contingent solely on trusting in Jesus Christ, it is impossible for any of us to save ourselves. On the crucifixion, Jesus made the ultimate sacrifice for our sins, and our salvation is contingent upon His death as well as his subsequent resurrection from the dead.

Finally, the Bible reminds us that the only people who can be saved are the ones who voluntarily embrace it. According to *John 3:16*,

Free-Falling Into Hell

"Because God so loved the world, He gave His only begotten Son, so that whomever believes in Him may not perish but have everlasting life," God gave His only son so that anyone who believe in him would not perish but would have eternal life. This text tells us that salvation is only available to those who voluntarily accept it by believing in Jesus and trusting in His death and resurrection for the forgiveness of their sins.

Those who do not believe in Jesus or trust in His death and resurrection will not be saved. God has given every one of us the ability to choose whether or not we want to be saved. In order for any of us to be saved, we need to first believe in Jesus Christ, then publicly declare that belief, and finally take up His offer of free salvation. Even though we cannot save ourselves, we nevertheless have the ability to make the correct choice by deciding whether or not to embrace the gift of salvation that God has provided for us free of charge.

How do we attain our salvation?

There's only one way to obtain salvation and that is by putting our faith in the shed blood of Jesus Christ, His death, burial and resurrection. If you confess Jesus Christ as Lord, believe in your heart that God raised Him from the dead, you shall be saved.

How do we remain in our Salvation?

Believing, remaining faithful, and obedient is what keeps us saved. Also, you must have a personal relationship with Jesus. By that, you have entered into the relationship with God that He calls everyone to and the Word of God provides us with everything we need to maintain that relationship. God provides us with His Word for our edification and our guidance. Consequently, we should make the Word a central part of our lives so that by it we weigh our words and actions.

In this manner, the Word should be ever-present to help guard us from sin: *Psalm. 119:11* (NIV) says, "I have hidden Your word in my heart that I might not sin against You." In addition to the purposes of initial regeneration and maintaining the closeness of our relationship with God, the Word exists to help us mature and grow in that relationship. This means that through His Word, God reveals Himself to us. Thus, the continual exposure to God through prayer, worship, and the Word washes us clean like the polishing of a dirty mirror. The more we are exposed to the washing of the Word, the better we are able to reflect God's character and image. Our change of lifestyle is a part of understanding that we have salvation.

How do we lose our Salvation?

There is no way you can lose your salvation if you did not have salvation from the start. It's not sinning that is going to cause us to lose our salvation. Just like it's not doing the right things that are going to earn us our salvation. It's a free gift from God. Can you reject that gift? Yes, you can reject that gift.

The reason you don't lose your salvation is because you were never saved in the first place. People may say they have salvation, but they never had a saving knowledge of Christ. You're always saved and have eternal security when you belong to Christ. But there are those who have only "tasted" or "sampled" Christ. They were never truly converted to faith in Him. There are many people who are involved, perhaps heavily involved in a church. It is likely they would have joined a congregation, heard the Gospel, and saw the Spirit working in the life of believers. They may have received some of the blessings of being part of a church, and they may have even publicly confessed Christ and have been baptized. But they never had a saving knowledge of Christ.

Free-Falling Into Hell

A good analogy would be the difference between marrying someone and just going out on a few dates with them. A person can learn things about Christ, and thereby come to admire Him, and they may enjoy being part of a fellowship but have no real lasting commitment to Him. This is not the same thing as the repentance and faith by which a person is saved and joined to Christ.

This is not an uncommon situation, there are people who have been in a church for many years, involved in many things, never missed a service, yet they are not saved. They have seen God at work, but only just "tasted" what was going on, never really being a part of it. They most likely would have even partaken of the Lord's Supper as the wording in the passage suggests. But they were never really saved. To sort of paraphrase Scripture, they were *"in the church, but not of the Church."*

So being a member of a church and be being involved in the Church and seeing God at work doesn't guarantee salvation. Neither does being baptized, for that matter. That is only what is called a "temporary faith". Temporary faith is most likely grounded in emotional feelings and seeks personal enjoyment rather than the glory of God.

There was a member in a church who was there for almost 40 years. He was a treasurer of the church. A very good outstanding member and never missed church. One night at church there was an altar call and to everybody's amazement, he got up went to the front and accepted the Lord as his personal Savior. Everyone was surprised because they thought that he was already a Christian and already saved all those years. Anybody can say they are a Christian and go through the motions of being a Christian but have never been saved in the first place.

That's why it is not difficult to understand why this kind of false faith is quickly lost when God or the church ceases to be fun and loses its appeal.

Free-Falling Into Hell

Unlike saving faith, temporary faith, "is not rooted in a regenerate heart." We find temporary faith in God's word in *Matthew 13:18-23* (NKJV):

The Parable of the Sower Explained

Matthew 13:18-23 (NKJV) says, "*Therefore hear the parable of the sower: When anyone hears the word of the kingdom, and does not understand it, then the wicked one comes and snatches away what was sown in his heart. This is he who received seed by the wayside. But he who received the seed on stony places, this is he who hears the word and immediately receives it with joy; yet he has no root in himself, but endures only for a while. For when tribulation or persecution arises because of the word, immediately he stumbles. Now he who received seed among the thorns is he who hears the word, and the cares of this world and the deceitfulness of riches choke the word, and he becomes unfruitful. But he who received seed on the good ground is he who hears the word and understands it, who indeed bears fruit and produces: some a hundredfold, some sixty, some thirty."*

That's what they have "fallen away" from the Visible Church, not salvation. Salvation is final as repentance is a gift of the Lord. Once you have been adopted into God's family, God will not let go. In *John 10:27-28* (NKJV), Jesus states: "My sheep hear my voice, and I know them, and they follow me. And I give them eternal life, and they shall never perish; neither shall anyone snatch them out of my hand." Once we are saved, we have an eternal security that is final.

There is also a kind of falling away that is final too. We have to keep in mind that this is not just a simple falling away where they just don't go to church anymore but one in which a person fully renounces Christ. Once they fall away and put the things of Christ completely behind them, they simply won't ever be gifted with any degree of repentance again. Anyone who makes such a decision was never a member of the Invisible Church.

We can see that what happens when we don't continue to abide in Christ in *John 15:1*-7 (NKJV) which says; "I am the true vine, and my Father is the vine-dresser. Every branch in Me that does not bear fruit He takes away; and every branch that bears fruit He prunes, that it may bear more fruit. You are already clean because of the word which I have spoken to you. Abide in Me, and I in you. As the branch cannot bear fruit of itself, unless it abides in the vine, neither can you, unless you abide in Me. I am the vine, you are the branches. He who abides in Me, and I in him, bears much fruit; for without Me you can do nothing. If anyone does not abide in Me, he is cast out as a branch and is withered; and they gather them and throw them into the fire, and they are burned. If you abide in Me, and My words abide in you, you will ask what you desire, and it shall be done for you."

I would suggest to you that the Bible does not teach eternal salvation, although it sure would be nice if it did. The Bible warns Christians that they can "fall from grace" (*Gal. 5:1-5*), be "cut off" from salvation (*Rom. 11:18-22*), have their names removed from the Lamb's Book of Life (*Rev. 22:19*), by committing certain sins and not repenting of them (cf. *Eph. 5: 3-5; 1Cor. 6:9; Gal. 5:19, Rev. 21:6-8*).

In a chilling reminder of the possibility of losing salvation by separating oneself from Christ, Paul says, "*I drive my body and train it, for fear that, after having preached to others, I myself should become disqualified.*" (1 Cor. 9:27). (NASB)

Here are a couple of additional passages that pretty much spell out the fact that one can lose one's salvation:

Free-Falling Into Hell

Matt: 6:15, 19:21-35, 10:22-32 Luke 12:41-46, Colossians 1:22-23, Hebrews 3:6, 14 Rev. 2:10, 25-36, 3:1-5 2 Peter 2:20-22

These passages give a pretty strong witness to the fact that we can fall away and, if we do not repent and come back to Jesus, we could suffer the consequences for all eternity.

Reconciled With God

Adam and Eve were perfect in the garden with no sin to think of, but everything drastically changed when the devil deceived Eve. The Serpent (the devil) lured Adam and Eve to eat the forbidden fruit from the tree of knowledge, and as a punishment for their disobedience, God banished them from the Garden of Eden. From Eden, the fellowship with God was broken. Adam lost that deep fellowship he had with God, but God never stopped loving him. So God wanted to regain the lost fellowship that he once had with Adam. Hence, He devised a method to regain the lost fellowship through the Ten Commandments. Even then, God knew that man would not be able to keep all of the commandments.

The Ten Commandments represent God's personal interest in bringing out the best in His children so that they may live life to the fullest. "The thief does not come except to steal, and to kill, and to destroy. I have come that they may have life, and that they may have it more abundantly" (*John 10:10* NKJV). The Commandments set God's people apart, identify right from wrong, and uphold the ultimate importance of love for God and neighbor in promoting peace in this life and salvation after.

God sets up sacrifices. The symbolism of animal sacrifice in the Bible is a concrete expression of God's justice and grace simultaneously. It reminded the Israelites of the serious nature of sin and its consequences for the individuals involved. These atoning sacrifices were how God would deal with the Israelites' sin and provide a reliable system the Israelites could use to maintain their right relationship with Him when they did sin. Animal sacrifices were commanded by God so that the individual could experience forgiveness of sin. The animal served as a substitute, that is, the animal died in place of the sinner, but only temporarily, which is why the sacrifices needed to be offered over and over.

With the arrival of Jesus Christ, animal sacrifices came to an end. Jesus Christ was the ultimate sacrificial substitute once for all time (*Hebrews 7:27*) and is now the only mediator between God and humanity (*1 Timothy 2:5*). Animal sacrifices foreshadowed Christ's sacrifice on our behalf. The only basis on which an animal sacrifice could provide forgiveness of sins is Christ, who would sacrifice Himself for our sins, providing the forgiveness that animal sacrifices could only illustrate and foreshadow. Original sin, in Christian doctrine, is the condition or state of sin into which each human being is born, also known as the origin sin (the cause or source) of this state.

Traditionally, the origin has been ascribed to the sin of the first man, Adam, who disobeyed God in eating the forbidden fruit (of knowledge of good and evil) and, consequently, transmitted his sin and guilt by heredity to his descendants. The doctrine has its basis in the Bible. Although the human condition (suffering, death, and a universal tendency toward sin) is accounted for by the story of the Fall of Adam in the early chapters of the book of Genesis, the main scriptural affirmation of the doctrine is found in the writings of Paul and particularly in *Romans 5:12-19*, which says:

"Therefore, just as through one man sin entered the world, and death through sin, and thus death spread to all men, because all sinned-- (For until the law sin was in the world, but sin is not imputed when there is no law. Nevertheless death reigned from Adam to Moses, even over those who had not sinned according to the likeness of the transgression of Adam, who is a type of Him who was to come. But the free gift is not like the offense. For if by the one man's offense many died, much more the grace of God and the gift by the grace of the one Man, Jesus Christ, abounded to many. And

the gift is not like that which came through the one who sinned. For the judgment which came from one offense resulted in condemnation, but the free gift which came from many offenses resulted in justification. For if by the one man's offense death reigned through the one, much more those who receive abundance of grace and of the gift of righteousness will reign in life through the One, Jesus Christ.) Therefore, as through one man's offense judgment came to all men, resulting in condemnation, even so through one Man's righteous act the free gift came to all men, resulting in justification of life. For as by one man's disobedience many were made sinners, so also by one Man's obedience many will be made righteous"
Romans 5:12-19, NKJV

This reflects a difficult passage in which Paul establishes a parallelism between Adam and Christ, stating that; although Adam brought sin and death into the world, Christ brought grace and eternal life in greater abundance. Before Jesus was born, the only way to God was through animal sacrifices and keeping the laws, which were the Ten Commandments. Just as a loving parent lays down ground rules for his child to follow to lead a safe and successful life, God the Father gave us the Ten Commandments to help us lead our best lives concerning our relationship with Him and with each other.

Since the Garden of Eden, man has rebelled against God. To help free humanity from this propensity to sin and to help each of us lead our best lives, God handed down the Ten Commandments as a code of moral laws for us to live by. In the first century before Christ's death, John the Baptist baptized in the wilderness and preached the baptism of repentance for the remission of sins, as the scripture says in (*Mark 1:4* NKJV), "John came baptizing in the wilderness and preaching a baptism of repentance for the remission of sins."

Certainly, Jesus Himself forgave sins during His personal ministry.

"When Jesus saw their faith, He said to the paralytic, "Son, your sins are forgiven you." And some of the scribes were sitting there and reasoning in their hearts, "Why does this Man speak blasphemies like this? Who can forgive sins but God alone?" But immediately, when Jesus perceived in His spirit what they reasoned within themselves, He said to them, "Why do you reason about these things in your hearts? Which is easier, to say to the paralytic, 'Your sins are forgiven you,' or to say, 'Arise, take up your bed and walk'? But that you may know that the Son of Man has power on earth to forgive sins, He said to the paralytic, "I say to you, arise, take up your bed, and go to your house." (*Mark 2:5-11* NKJV).

And yet Paul writes, "When the fullness of the time came, God sent forth his Son, born of a woman, born under the law, that he might redeem them that were under the law" (*Galatians 4:4-5*). How can one text indicate there was forgiveness before the death of Christ, while other texts clearly state that there was no pardon of sin until after the death of Christ? The Ten Commandments are not an onerous set of rules we should follow out of fear or guilt. Rather, the Commandments serve as a signposts that point us to the straight and narrow path while showing us our need for a Savior when we inevitably stray from that path. Under the Law of Moses, the priests made animal sacrifices and burned them upon the altar for a sweet savor unto Jehovah;

"and the priest shall make atonement from him, and he shall be forgiven. "He shall remove all its fat, as fat is removed from the sacrifice of the peace offering; and the priest shall burn it on the altar for a sweet aroma to the LORD. So the priest shall make atonement for him, and it shall be forgiven him" (*Leviticus 4:31* NKJV).

Animal sacrifices foreshadowed Christ's sacrifice on our behalf. The only basis on which an animal sacrifice could provide forgiveness of sins is Christ, who would sacrifice Himself for our sins, providing the forgiveness that animal sacrifices could only illustrate and foreshadow. The answer lies in understanding the nature of the word "forgiveness."

There could never have been forgiveness of sin without sufficient propitiation given for man's sins. This could only have come through the shedding of blood (*Hebrews 9:22*). But it is impossible that the blood of bulls and goats should take away sins (*Hebrews 10:4*). It took, therefore, the sacrificial death of God's Son. Only then could God remain just and the justifier of the one who has faith in Jesus.

"For all have sinned and fall short of the glory of God, being justified freely by His grace through the redemption that is in Christ Jesus, whom God set forth as a propitiation by His blood, through faith, to demonstrate His righteousness, because in His forbearance God had passed over the sins that were previously committed, to demonstrate at the present time His righteousness, that He might be just and the justifier of the one who has faith in Jesus" (*Romans 3:23-26* NKJV).

The only way anyone, regardless of what point in time they live, can be forgiven of sin and stand justified in the sight of God is through God's grace. "For by grace you have been saved through faith, and that not of yourselves; it is the gift of God," (*Ephesians 2:8* NKJV). Therefore, having been justified by faith, we have peace with God through our Lord Jesus Christ.

This is confirmed in *Romans 5:2* which says: "Through whom also we have access by faith into this grace in which we stand, and rejoice in hope of the glory of God." The fact is, all who lived before

Christ's death reached salvation by grace through faith, just like those saved after Christ's sacrificial death.

The writer of the book of Hebrews makes this point in chapter eleven of as he lists many in both the Patriarchal and Mosaic era that were saved by their faith; a faith which, by the way, was made complete through obedience. "These all died in faith, not having received the promises, but having seen them afar off were assured of them, embraced them and confessed that they were strangers and pilgrims on the earth" (*Hebrews 11:13* NKJV). Those who died in faith before Christ's sacrificial death looked forward in time to the fulfillment of that promise, while the faith of all who have been forgiven after Christ's death looks backward to the cross.

God knew of the certainty of His promise of redemption. He knew that in the fullness of time, His Son would die for the sins of the world.

Therefore, on that basis and because of the immutability of His counsel, God could and did forgive the faithful of those previous dispensations. "Thus God, determining to show more abundantly to the heirs of promise the immutability of His counsel, confirmed it by an oath," (*Hebrews 6:17* NKJV).

Prepare For The End

Most of us go from year-to-year without ever worrying about our life. But what happens when our time runs out and it will? There will be a time when our life will come to an end as we know it. Have you thought about, what will happen after you died? Majority of us remember that song "time is on my side "and, most of us take time for granted. We act like we have all the time in the world. But in reality nobody knows how much time we really have. It's only through God's mercy and grace that we have time.

Life is a vapor! Like a morning mist that soon vanishes, so life is short and uncertain. What if you only had one day to live? What would you do differently? Let's face it, we all live our lives like there's no tomorrow; we don't give it much thought, but there is no guarantee that we will see tomorrow. Tomorrow is not promised to us. People die every day, whether by accident or natural causes. When we go to sleep at night, we don't know if we will wake up the next morning. If we do wake up, we don't give much thought to our new day and what the end result of that day will be. We just prepare ourselves to go on with our normal daily routine.

Nobody knows how much time we have, the Bible speaks of our life being like a vapor, it's here one minute and it's gone in the next. We need to prepare ourselves when the time comes for us to end this life given to us by God. Do you know where you will be when your life comes to an end? Most of us don't want to deal with or think about death. But it is inevitable that we will all see death at some point of our lives. Death is not a laughing matter; it is something that we need to think about. Will you be prepared when death comes knocking at your door?

We can make the decision to turn to God only as we live and breathe. Once our breath is gone and we expire, we have no more choices and we have to be accountable to God. Where do you want to spend eternity? The choice is yours! You need to turn to Jesus and allow him to come into your heart while you still have the breath of life.

Most of us know what an hour glass is. It's full of sand and when you turn it upside down the sand starts to fall immediately without stopping. That's the way it is with our lives. When we start our life, it goes on continuously until death comes. And the Bible teaches that we will either go to heaven or to hell at death.

Many think that we have all the time in the world because there is no end to this world as we know it. We live and die and that's the end of it. They don't believe that there is a God or that Hell, even exists, much less Heaven. How can you be sure that there is no Hell or Heaven? And if by chance you do believe in a heaven, how can you make sure that you'll spend eternity there?

Free-Falling Into Hell

Preparation is essential to every endeavor. We prepare for retirement, for a trip, for the children's college, for a job, and the list goes on. But we don't seem to see the need for making preparation for the greatest of all events: that of life after death! We will meet God, prepared or not! So, don't let your life slip away without making the proper preparation to meet God in judgment. Then you can plan to live with Him throughout the ceaseless ages of eternity.

Most people think that they can earn their way into heaven by living a good life or by turning up to church every Sunday. But whatever our ancestry, background, or upbringing, whatever rituals and ceremonies we have performed, whatever religion, we have followed, however sincerely we have tried to live a good life, the same facts remain, we are spiritually dead until we turn to Jesus.

The truth is that none of these things makes us right with God. We are morally corrupt and guilty before God. We are powerless to save ourselves. Left as we are, our case is hopeless. Rather than rely on guesswork and what we think we need to achieve, God's word (the Bible) tells us how to have a relationship with God and a life that is lived to the fullest. Jesus tells us in the Bible that he has come, that we may have life, and may have it abundantly!

We can't do anything to earn our way into heaven, but the good news is that we don't have to. God sent Jesus into the world, and Jesus lived the way we were always meant to live. Jesus came to provide the only way by which we could be reunited with God. His innocent death took the punishment we deserved because of our rejection of God. Because Jesus has paid the price for us, he offers us salvation and eternal life. Make a decision to accept Jesus into your life and to share eternity with him.

God's salvation offer is eternal life through Jesus Christ his Son; forgiveness, and freedom from spiritual death. The truth will set you free.

Ephesians 2:1-10 (NIV)

"As for you, you were dead in your transgressions and sins, in which you used to live when you followed the ways of this world and of the ruler of the kingdom of the air, the spirit who is now at work in those who are disobedient. All of us also lived among them at one time, gratifying the cravings of our flesh, following its desires and thoughts. Like the rest, we were by nature deserving of wrath. But because of his great love for us, God, who is rich in mercy, made us alive with Christ even when we were dead in transgressions —it is by grace you have been saved. And God raised us up with Christ and seated us with him in the heavenly realms in Christ Jesus, so that in the coming ages he might show the incomparable riches of his grace, expressed in his kindness to us in Christ Jesus. For it is by grace and through faith that you have been saved. This is not for yourselves, it is the gift of God, not by works, so that no one can boast. For we are God's handiwork, created in Christ Jesus to do good works, which God prepared in advance for us to do."

The two steps in salvation are; hearing the gospel and believing it. Truly hearing and believing are what make up your faith. Hearing is fairly straightforward; we must hear the gospel because it is by hearing it that we are introduced to Jesus Christ. However, it is one thing to just hear the Gospel, and another thing to believe it.

Many Christians are fine with hearing God's Word, and even studying it, but many have a difficult time believing it. I think we know that we truly believe God's Word by the ways that takes shape in our lives, and by the transformation of our heart and mind. We act differently when we move from simply hearing, to accepting the Word.

During the earthly ministry of Jesus there were many people who did not believe Him yet He was performing miracles right in front of their eyes. Believing is a little more difficult because what it takes for a person to believe is based entirely on the conditional response of the person. Some people can believe based on hearing a sermon only, while others need to thoroughly research every detail. Neither of these positions is wrong, though they require different approaches.

Sometimes people tell us things that are too hard for us to believe. It's one thing to hear about something and another to believe it. Its one thing to hear the Gospel and then another to choose to reject it. In Acts 26 we find Paul defending himself and the Gospel. It is In this chapter that we find the most exhaustive defense of all of Paul's defenses recorded in the Book of Acts. He was telling King

Agrippa how he became a believer. King Agrippa said to Paul *"You almost persuade me to become a Christian."* King Agrippa is like most people who hear the gospel, yet they don't want to surrender their lives to Christ. It's like, they like what they are hearing but they are hard-pressed to believe because they don't want to change their lifestyle.

It takes preparation to conquer the disbelief that is ingrained in us. Preparation of our hearts and minds comes with reading the Word of God. The Word is true; we must come to the point where we believe it beyond a shadow of a doubt. To see the promises of God come to pass we believe His Word. We believe God's promises in the Word and by God's power they are brought to pass in our lives.

The word "believe" is a verb that connotes action. Therefore, believing the Word of God, taking the Word of God literally and acting upon it, brings results. This is the law of believing and this is the action that will bring release and victory to your life in every situation. You have to believe in God; in who He is; that he can do whatever he says he would do. Only by believing, all things will be available. For there is nothing impossible for God. Take a miracle for instance, if it didn't happen to you, you would be hard-pressed to believe it.

We can hear the Word of God by listening to our pastor giving us the message or we can hear by reading the Word. Both ways are excellent ways of learning about the Lord and believing the truth.

This world and this world's kingdoms are under the domain of Satan (*Ephesians 6:12*). Satan is presently called the "god of this world" (*2 Corinthians 4:4*). Even Jesus refers to this world kingdom belonging to Satan in (*Matthew 12:26*). Because of the fall of man and because of this act of disobedience, all mankind has a sinful nature. *Romans 5:12* (NKJV) says; "Therefore, just as through one man sin entered the world, and death through sin, and thus death spread to all men, because all sinned."

We once were of this world and a friend with the devil. But now we belong to God and are a friend of God. The devil does not like losing his own and will try every trick he knows to turn you away from God. That's were spiritual warfare comes in.

We need to be an example to our friends, neighbors, and the strangers down the street, that they would want what they see in us. We changed from a life of destruction to a life of eternal joy! Satan will do whatever it takes to keep this world in darkness. He is totally against anything that God has planned for us. He is a great imitator of what God does but always in the opposite direction against God.

Have you ever been inside a candy store? You see all these different kinds of candies and goodies and they all look so good and tempting. They are made that way so they can catch your attention and you will buy some. The world can be seen in the same way, as having many different kinds of pleasures to tempt you. But we need to remember that everything of the world will only leads you away from God.

Jesus who lived and dined among sinners was a very good example as to how we should be. We are not to isolate ourselves from the world, we are to live here with the ungodly people. We should not be like the monks who withdrew and isolated themselves from the mainline society during the Middle Ages or Medieval Times. They were a poor testimony to Christ. They kept to themselves instead of going out and spreading the Gospel to help those in darkness. We must live together as the parable of the wheat and tares that Jesus outlined for us in *Matthew 13:24-30* (NKJV) states.

The world is in darkness because of sin and whoever is born of this world has a sinful nature. So we must be a light that shines in the darkness to help those who are blinded by this world and living in darkness to see the light of Christ. Christians who separate themselves from the world and seek to escape it do not know Christ. As Christians we must live among the people who live in darkness in this fallen world so that our light will shine in the darkness, for light exposes darkness.

Therefore, as Christians our outward life should reflect our inward life. The work that the Holy Spirit has done inside us should come out for the world to see that they may glorify our heavenly father. We live around sinful people, though we don't have sinful partnership or fellowship with them. We do not partake in their unfruitful deeds of darkness for God has delivered us from the power darkness.

We must also understand that being in the world, but not of it, is necessary if we are to be a light to those who are in spiritual darkness. We are to live in such a way that those outside the faith see our good deeds and our manner and know that there is something different about us. Being in the world also means we can enjoy the things of the world such as the beautiful creation God has given us. But we are not to immerse ourselves in what the world values, nor are we to chase after worldly pleasures.

Worldly pleasures are no longer our calling in life as it once was but we must pursue Godly pleasures. As Christians we can have wants and needs; God wants to bless us and to live an abundant life. So let your light shine ever so brightly as the guiding light, that hope is seen through you. Let your light be: BRIGHT, BEAUTIFUL, and DESIRABLE.

Matthew 5:14-16 (NKJV) says; *"You are the light of the world. A city that is set on a hill cannot be hidden. Nor do they light a lamp and put it under a basket, but on a lampstand, and it gives light to all who are in the house. Let your light so shine before men, that they may see your good works and glorify your Father in heaven."*

The Wiles of Satan

Satan would have you be ignorant about his existence, because it is to Satan's advantage to have his presence denied. He would be able to work in secret when it came to deceiving mankind. Satan originated his own sin and will use anything to mislead you away from God. He uses the Scriptures as he did when he tempted Jesus Christ. Christ defeated Satan in the wilderness. Satan only uses half-truths, which have just enough truth in them to trick us.

Satan is a murder; he will rather see us dead then to see us turn to Christ. He is the originator of sin and sin is what brings death, so by tempting us he is pronouncing a death sentence upon us. *John 8:44* (RSV) says; "You are of your father the devil, and your will is to do your father's desires. He was a murderer from the beginning, and has nothing to do with the truth, because there is no truth in him.

When he lies, he speaks according to his own nature, for he is a liar and the father of lies."

The Bible warns us of the deceptions of Satan. He can transform himself into an Angel of light. That could be deceiving, if you are not in the word of God daily. Only spiritual maturity can protect us from Satan, the master of deceit. *Ephesians 4:27* (TMSG) states; "Don't give the Devil that kind of foothold in your life."

He uses whosoever listens to him even people in church offices to deceive God's people. The apostle Paul spoke of false prophets who misled the churches they worked with. Those false prophets or instruments of Satan as we should call them have no part in our Christian hope. That is why it's so important for us as Christians to stay in the word daily, so that we won't be deceived. Satan is an imitator or, I should say a copycat of everything that God tries to do. God has apostles, prophets, evangelist, ministers or pastors, and teachers so Satan tries to have the same.

2 Corinthians 11:13 - 15 (NKJV) says; "For such are false apostles, deceitful workers, transforming themselves into apostles of Christ. And no wonder! For Satan himself transforms himself into an angel of light. Therefore it is no great thing if his ministers also transform themselves you into ministers of righteousness, whose end will be according to their works."

Gods Plan: Repent, Salvation, Faith, Hope, Love.

Satan's Plan: Doubt, Discouragement, Division, Defeat, Delay.

Satan seeks to deceive us. His target is our mind. He will try to plant a seed in our minds and if we allow it to take hold, it may lead us to sin. We must always keep our minds clear that is why Jesus said, *"don't be drunk with wine."* When we are drunk we have no control of our minds. So it is very important not to allow any imaginations in our minds. When we fill our minds with the word of God there is no room for evil imaginations to take place. It's very important to always stay in the word of God. Be filled with the Holy Spirit and it will leave no room for the flesh.

Satan gets us to entertain fantasies, because he knows that the fantasies often turn into reality. The wrong imaginations are like a pregnancy, it grows in your mind and as we continue feeding the fantasy in our mind the more it grows until we birth sin.

2 Corinthians 11:3 (NKJV) says; "But I fear, lest somehow, as the serpent deceived Eve by his craftiness, so your minds may be corrupted from the simplicity that is in Christ."

If Satan is successful in getting us to think wrongly about God and salvation, then he can corrupt our effectiveness as believers in our relationship with God. Therefore, it is imperative that we are rooted in God's truth through his word and prayer. Our effectiveness as believer's stems directly from the facts that we are made righteous through the redemptive work of Christ's at Calvary, and not by our own works. The bible says in *Philippians 3:9* (NKJV) that; *"and be found in Him, not having my own righteousness, which is from the law, but that which is through faith in Christ, the righteousness which is from God by faith;"*

I remember my daughter telling me once that when she prayed at night before going to sleep, she would have a hard time sleeping. The times that she didn't pray she slept good. Satan leaves us alone when we belong to him and doing the things of the world. But when we are in fellowship with God, the devil tries whatever he can to bring us down to his level. Satan will never appear to us, as he is a spirit of pure wickedness full of evil and deceit. He is the Prince of Duplicity and is able to assume any character. The only way he can tempt us is by having a great appearance of virtue and religion.

An Angel of light appeared to both Mohammad and Joseph Smith as they both claimed. Each wrote their own interpretation of the Bible, Joseph Smith, the book of Mormon's and Mohammad, the Koran. The devil is a very cunning evil spirit and will use any means possible to deceive people into going the opposite of God's direction. The devil even tried to tempt Jesus.

Spirit inspired men who were led by the Holy Spirit wrote the Bible. There were many men and not one man like Mohammad who wrote the Koran and one man like Joseph Smith who wrote the book of Mormon. 2 *Corinthians 11:14 - 15* (NLT) says; "But I am not surprised! Even Satan disguises himself as an angel of light. So it is no wonder that his servants also disguise themselves as servants of righteousness. In the end they will get the punishment their wicked deeds deserve."

Only spiritual maturity and insight can protect us from the master of deceit, the devil. He will lead you away from God; he is a liar and a cheat and will try to kill you before you surrender to Jesus. When you belong to the world and are doing things of the world. Satan has no need to interfere in your life, because you already belong to him. It is not until you decide to leave the things of the world and follow Christ that he starts coming around and tries to turn you back to the ways of the world.

Life can be difficult as a Christian, because you will always have Satan trying to rob you of your blessings from God. That is why it's very important that we are rooted deeply in our faith. You must remember that Satan is already spiritually dead and will not be reconciled with God. He has nothing to lose since he already lost his place with God. He is trying to deceive mankind into believing that there is no God. Just by looking around us we do see the beauty of the Lord. Nothing evil could have created this beautiful earth. The Bible tells us that the just must live by faith. *Romans 1:17* (NKJV) says; "For in it the righteousness of God is revealed from faith to faith; as it is written, "The just shall live by faith."

As Christians we need to live by every word in the Bible. There will always be questions as to how things happen or why things happen. As Christians that should not be our concern, we should only be concerned with following Christ's direction. God gave us a mind that we can think and in that mind he also instilled conscience, mercy, and passion. We need to lean on God's understanding and not our own understanding. We are but a small pea in the pot compared to the vastness of God. We should be asking ourselves; *why must we question everything, instead of just trusting and leaning on God?* God is not a man that he should lie, when we become Christians the Holy Spirit, which is God, comes and dwells in us.

1 Corinthians 3:16 (TMSG) says; " You realize, don't you, that you are the temple of God, and God himself is present in you?"

When Jesus was on earth he was fully man and fully God. He also said greater things; which we will do because of him going to the father. God our father is the one that provides the anointing. That would mean that nothing is impossible for us as long as we believe in what we say or ask for in faith, and knowing it will be done, without any doubt in our minds.

Doubt is a Christian's worst enemy and is one of Satan's tools. *Matthew 21:21* (NKJV) reads; *"So Jesus answered and said to them, "Assuredly, I say to you, if you have faith and do not doubt, you will not only do what was done to the fig tree, but also if you say to this mountain, 'Be removed and be cast into the sea,' it will be done."*

As genuine Christians we must only walk by faith and not by sight. Does Satan exist? The answer

Free-Falling Into Hell

is **YES**. He has been around since he was thrown out of heaven; he just stays out of sight, but not out of you mind, so don't give him the opportunity to come into your mind.

Choose Life: Choose Christ

James 4:13-14 (NKJV)

"Come now, you who say, "Today or tomorrow we will go to such and such a city, spend a year there, buy and sell, and make a profit;" whereas you do not know what will happen tomorrow. For what is your life? It is even a vapor that appears for a little time and then vanishes away."

Most of us don't want to deal with or think about death. But it is inevitable that we will all see death at some point of our lives.

The Fork of Life

A fork in the road is a metaphor, based on a literal expression, for a deciding moment in life or history when a major choice of options is required. As newborns, we are cared for by our parents because we are too young to make decisions on our own. But there will be a time when we get to the age of reasoning and begin to be morally responsible. This is when we will come to the crossroads of life. Everyone comes to the crossroads and must choose which road to take.

Right side: The narrow way through Jesus Christ, the way of the cross. It may be rocky and narrow, and it will never merge with the crowded superhighway nudging the masses toward a global village. But no other way leads to genuine love, peace, and lasting security. The destination is well worth the struggle.

Left side: A broad road to destruction, the way of the world, where everything seems like fun and games. Jesus warns us that the larger masses of people will go down the broad road to destruction.

Most people will reject God's way of life, because of all the sorrow and suffering. The Lord urges us to enter the narrow gate. Few find it, even though it leads to eternal life. One should strive to find the narrow way through Jesus Christ.

Those who seek the Lord will find the way. The narrow gate and road refers to Jesus' teaching, which emphasizes not on external requirements, but internal transformation; being born again in the spirit, as Jesus explained to Nicodemus.

John 3:3-8 (NKJV) says; "Jesus answered and said to him, Most assuredly, I say to you, unless one is born again, he cannot see the kingdom of God. Nicodemus said to Him, "How can a man be born when he is old? Can he enter a second time into his mother's womb and be born?" Jesus answered, "Most assuredly, I say to you, unless one is born of water and the Spirit, he cannot enter the kingdom of God. That which is born of the flesh is flesh, and that which is born of the Spirit is spirit. Do not marvel that I said to you, 'You must be born again.' The wind blows where it wishes, and you hear the sound of it, but cannot tell where it comes from and where it goes. So is everyone who is born of the Spirit.""

Free-Falling Into Hell

The call of the Holy Spirit is to all, to enter the narrow gate. The doors to the kingdom of God are always open. *Revelation 3:20* (NKJV) says; "Behold, I stand at the door and knock. If anyone hears My voice and opens the door, I will come in to him and dine with him, and he with Me." Even Jesus acknowledged that few would find the true way, the way that leads to eternal life. *Matthew 7:13-14* (NKJV) reads; "Enter by the narrow gate; for wide is the gate and broad is the way that leads to destruction, and there are many who go in by it. Because narrow is the gate and difficult is the way which leads to life, and there are few who find it.

Jesus presented the clear access to righteousness. Many will find out too late that the road they are traveling on leads to hell, and not heaven. If you were to die today, are you absolutely positive that you will go to heaven? Do you have eternal life? Contrary to popular belief, not all roads lead to heaven. *John 17:3* (ESV) says; "And this is eternal life, that they know you the only true God, and Jesus Christ whom you have sent." Knowing God is eternal life. When Jesus said eternal life was to know God, he meant having an intimate, close, personal relationship with God. What is Eternal Life? Eternal Life is: an Intimate relationship with God.

How do you make preparation for eternal life? The Bible offers five steps in preparing for eternity.

1. **Hearing the gospel.** *Matthew 4:23* (NKJV) says; "And Jesus went about all Galilee, teaching in their synagogues, preaching the gospel of the kingdom, and healing all kinds of sickness and all kinds of disease among the people."

2. **Believing or having faith.** The bible says in *John 8:23-24* (NKJV) that; *"And He said to them, "You are from beneath; I am from above. You are of this world; I am not of this world.*

Therefore I said to you that you will die in your sins; for if you do not believe that I am He, you will die in your sins."

3. **Repentance:** It involves a change of mind that results in a change of life._*Acts 17:30* (NKJV) says; *"Truly, these times of ignorance God overlooked, but now commands all men everywhere to repent,"*

4. **Get ready:** No one will go to heaven by accident; but by preparing to go. The parable of the wise and foolish virgins teaches us in (*Matthew. 25:1-13*) that only *"they that were ready went in."*

As God challenged Israel of old, "prepare to meet thy God, O Israel" (Amos 4:12), he challenges us today. We will meet God, prepared or not! So, don't let your life slip away without making the proper preparation to meet God in judgment. Then you can plan to live with Him throughout the ceaseless ages of eternity. Matthew 25:46

(NKJV) says; "And these will go away into everlasting punishment, but the righteous into eternal life."

An open Invitation

No matter where you are in life, it's not too late to turn to God. God calls everyone.

Acts 17:30 (NKJV) "Truly, these times of ignorance God overlooked, but now commands all men everywhere to repent."

1 Corinthians 1:9 (NKJV) "God is faithful, by whom you were called into the fellowship of His Son, Jesus Christ our Lord."

God calls you to become the person He created you to be and to do the things He designed you to do. The Bible teaches that the Lord must draw men and women to Himself in faith since we are unable to do so on our own.

John 6:44 (NKJV), "No one can come to Me unless the Father who sent Me draws him; and I will raise him up at the last day."

Isaiah 1:18 (NKJV), "Come now, and let us reason together," Says the LORD, "Though your sins are like scarlet, they shall be as white as snow; Though they are red like crimson, they shall be as wool."

You have an open invitation from the Lord, but it is only valid as long as we are alive. Once we die, we either face eternal damnation or eternal life with Christ. Choose now who's going to be your master; the prince of this world or the King to come. For once you die; it's too late!

The Holy Spirit

An essential part of becoming a Christian is turning away from sin and turning to God We must repent from our old ways of life. This is only possible when God works in us to will and to do His will.

When you become a Christian, God comes and lives inside you through his Holy Spirit. The Holy Spirit comes and regenerates your spirit. This is called being "born again." The Holy Spirit will teach you all truth and give you the power to choose right over wrong. You are restored to a relationship with God, God becomes your Father, and you become His child, fit to inherit His Kingdom.

2 Thessalonians 2:13 (NKJV), "But we are bound to give thanks to God always for you, brethren beloved by the Lord because God from the beginning chose you for salvation through sanctification by the Spirit and belief in the truth,"

Be Persuaded

Consider King Agrippa in Paul's last recorded testimony in his many trials. You can read the entire story in Acts 26. Near the end of the chapter, we read;

"For the king, before whom I also speak freely, knows these things; for I am convinced that none of these things escapes his attention, since this thing was not done in a corner. King Agrippa, do you believe the prophets? I know that you do believe." Then Agrippa said to Paul, "You almost persuade me to become a Christian." And Paul said, "I would to God that not only you, but also all who hear me today, might become both almost and altogether such as I am, except for these chains." Acts 26:26-29 (NKJV)

In this testimony, Paul addresses king Agrippa as well as all the listeners. At the end he calls the king to declare his faith in the prophets and by extension, the Messiah about whom the prophets had spoken. Agrippa was convicted, he believed and wanted Christ but he didn't accept him, either to save face or with the hope of a better time. He was almost persuaded. But to be almost persuaded, dear reader, is to be totally lost. Unfortunately, many today are almost persuaded. They do not realize that today is the accepted hour, today is the time of their salvation for tomorrow, while hoped for, is not guaranteed.

Dear reader, we have no other hope but in Christ, no other way but through Christ, and no other choice except Christ. Accept Him today in your life as your Lord and Savior.

Choose Life, Choose Christ.

www.ingramcontent.com/pod-product-compliance
Lightning Source LLC
Chambersburg PA
CBHW051319120626
46547CB00015B/2301